P9-CCS-016

HALF-TRUTHS AND BRAZEN LIES
AN HONEST LOOK AT LYING

by **Kira Vermond**

Illustrated by **Clayton Hanmer**

Owlkids Books

Contents

INTRODUCTION

Do you believe in telling the truth? Sure you do.

Then you might as well admit it: You LIE!

Relax. Given the right conditions, we all lie. Everybody. Friends, teachers, athletes, movie stars, doctors, scientists…gasp, even your parents. Lying is as much a part of us as our curiosity. It's central to human nature. In other words, we tell fibs, corkers, fictions, falsehoods, and tall tales because we just can't help ourselves.

Here's something else: We lie a *lot*. One study found that six out of every ten people lied at least once during a ten-minute conversation. Most of them didn't even realize they were doing it!

Honest to goodness

It's strange that we treat lying differently from many of our other universal, shared traits. Unlike eating, sleeping, and crying, lying is commonly held to be bad. It's immoral—wicked.

But is it? Here are a few questions for you:

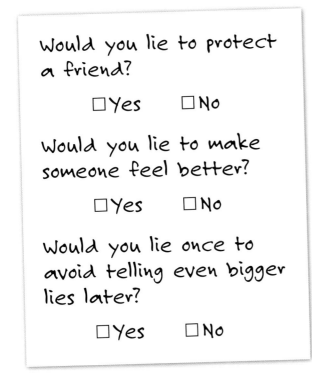

Would you lie to protect a friend?

☐ Yes ☐ No

Would you lie to make someone feel better?

☐ Yes ☐ No

Would you lie once to avoid telling even bigger lies later?

☐ Yes ☐ No

Mixed messages

How did you answer? Though many lies are immoral, hurtful, or unethical, some certainly are not. There are experts who say lies are actually so necessary that society would collapse if we told the truth all the time. Some types of lies help communities run more smoothly and make people happier.

You were probably taught that honesty is the best policy. So why do your parents ask you to pretend you like *all* your birthday gifts, even Aunt Dora's knitted dinosaur sweater? Does "being polite" mean lying? And aren't card players encouraged to bluff when they play poker? Talk about mixed messages!

So lies = good? Before you get too excited, it's still uncool to spread false stories about other kids. Or to tell your parents that you're studying when you're actually playing a video game. These lies can be hurtful, and they're not so good for you, either.

Luckily, there are ways to tell the difference between good fibs, bad lies, and untruths that fall into a large gray zone. Keep reading because there is much to learn about lies and deception. Honest!

Chapter 1

WHAT'S IN A LIE?

TRUE STORY

"There's nothing like real homegrown spaghetti…"

When British families plopped down in front of their television sets one night in 1957, they thought they were in for some regular old TV viewing. *Panorama*, a popular BBC news show, was on.

Toward the end of the show, the news anchor turned to the camera and said, "We end *Panorama* tonight with a special report from the Swiss Alps."

The footage showed Switzerland in springtime and women wearing traditional Swiss clothing—plucking long strands of spaghetti from trees!

"The last two weeks of March are an anxious time for the spaghetti farmer," the reporter explained, with a straight face.

While he spoke, so-called farmers were shown spreading out a harvest of fresh spaghetti to dry in the sun. Viewers were told that the threat of frost could ruin the pasta's taste, but at least the dreaded "spaghetti weevil" insect hadn't damaged the crops that year.

When the story was over, the anchor finished the broadcast by saying, "Now we say good night… on this first day of April."

Of course, the story wasn't true. It was an April Fools' Day joke told for fun. But not many people in Britain knew that at the time. Italian pasta was still considered a special, exotic dish.

Hundreds of viewers called in to the station to ask where they could buy a spaghetti bush! Others wanted to know how to grow their own tree. The reply?

"Place a sprig of spaghetti in a tin of tomato sauce and hope for the best."

Hoaxes pocus

So is an April Fools' Day joke actually a lie? Sure, though not the same kind you might tell to wriggle out of an uncomfortable situation. The spaghetti joke was considered a hoax. A really good one, too.

> An April Fools' hoax is a special kind of lie that's…
> - outrageous
> - told in good fun
> - meant to grab the public's attention

Perhaps what really sets a hoax apart from other kinds of lies is that the liar *wants* to be found out…eventually. Many companies now make up elaborate April Fools' Day hoaxes to get attention and publicity, only to reveal the truth later. For instance, on April 1, 2014, Domino's Pizza UK claimed it was now offering an edible pizza box, calling it the "future of snackaging." Meanwhile, Sonic Drive-In, the American fast-food restaurant, declared it would soon be offering a kale cream pie shake. Back in 2011, Canadian airline WestJet released a video stating that the company would be adding helium (think of helium balloons) to their planes to make them lighter! It was all a bunch of hot air, of course.

As hoaxes show, there are many different kinds of lies and lots of reasons people tell them. This chapter is about answering the question: When is a lie a lie—and when is it something else?

WHEN IS A LIE A LIE?

What's worse than being called a liar? Being called a liar when you thought you were telling the truth! Maybe it's time everyone gets a lesson on what the word "lie" actually means.

Warning! The following definition seems simple, but it's a head-exploding brainteaser that philosophers (big thinkers who study human beliefs) have been debating for centuries.

Here's the standard definition that (most) people agree on now:

EXHIBIT A

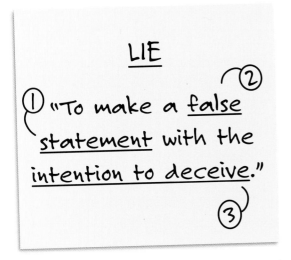

LIE

① "To make a ② false statement with the intention to deceive." ③

① It's a statement. You have to communicate a thought either by speaking or by writing it down.

② It has to be untrue.

③ The liar has to be trying to trick another person.

That's simple enough

Sure, the definition seems super handy when you're trying to figure out if someone is lying or not. For example...

Pretending

"You're a robot and I'm an alien, and we're going to make a sandcastle."

These kids are **saying** something **untrue**, but because they both are in on the ruse, there's **no deception**.

Verdict: Not a lie!

Nobody believes your lie

"I didn't eat the cookies. I swear!"

Even though you're a bad liar and no one is fooled, you are still trying to pull a fast one.

Verdict: Lie!

But, but, but...

Unfortunately, there are many gray areas and situations that don't quite fit the usual definition of lying.

You nod your head yes when you're really thinking no

Some philosophers believe that this isn't a lie because you're not speaking or writing a statement, but others say that's silly. Nodding counts because it communicates an idea.

You're being sarcastic

When your dad enters your messy room and says, "What a fresh smell and uncluttered sleeping area!" he obviously doesn't mean what he says, but is he lying? No. His tone of voice tells you what he's getting at despite his choice of words. There's no intention to deceive. (But he can quit it with his lame *conversational implicature*. Look that one up!)

You think you're telling a lie, but it's actually the truth!

When your rival asks you what pages to study for tomorrow's math test, you give her the wrong ones. (Just so we're clear, this is *not* your best moment.) Except…it turns out you gave her the *correct* pages by accident, and she gets an A. Did you lie? Tricky one. You're making a statement and you're trying to deceive her, but—oops!—you told the truth. Some people would give you a free pass, but not everyone. There are experts who add something extra to the definition: Liars just have to *believe* that what they're saying is false—it doesn't matter if it's not!

Lies in disguise

Sometimes we like to S-T-R-E-T-C-H the meaning of lying to include things that aren't strictly the real deal, although they would still be considered deception.

Lies of omission:

you leave out important facts so you can mislead others

Cheating and stealing:

your action is deceptive

Exaggeration:

your facts are mostly true, but you add a few that aren't and stretch the truth

Forgery:

you create something phony that you hope people will mistake for the real deal

Fabrication:

you say something that you *think* is true, but you're not actually 100 percent sure

Plagiarism:

you copy someone else's work and pass it off as your own

Here's one more: lying to yourself. While some philosophers say the best liars often believe the lies they're telling on some level, others disagree. They think it's impossible to convince yourself to believe something false while knowing the truth at the same time. Either you know what's real or you don't.

LIES: HANDY OR HORRIBLE?

Now that we know what a lie is, how do we decide if lying is morally right? That is, how do we judge if it's good or bad to lie? Let's take a look at the upside and downside of deception.

EXHIBIT C

EXHIBIT B

Yay! Lies

• Lies work. They can get you what you want and even keep you out of trouble.

• Lies give us a layer of privacy so that we can keep some of our secret thoughts to ourselves.

• "Great-looking haircut!" Sometimes we tell lies to be kind or polite.

• Would you lie to save your little sister's life? How about your own? Sure. Most people agree that lying is justified if something terrible would happen otherwise.

Boo! Lies

• When someone lies to you, you aren't able to make a decision based on the truth. Sometimes that can lead to disaster.

• Ever been lied to? Feels crummy, doesn't it? Your faith is shattered, your trust is gone, and you might even be feeling pretty dumb for believing the person in the first place.

• Bending the truth puts pressure on liars, too. They have to keep track of their lies, remember who they lied to, and tell more lies to avoid detection.

• Caught in the act of lying? One big lie can hurt your credibility, or how much people will trust you from that point on.

• Some studies show that being dishonest hurts self-esteem and can even make you sick.

• Lies work—and that's the problem. Once one person lies, cheats, or deceives and gets away with it, others think, "I'll try that, too!" One lie can turn into a virus that spreads and spreads.

So what would a "liar, liar, pants on fire" society even look like?

Not pretty. Imagine a world where everybody lies all the time. Not little or unimportant lies, but big, hurtful whoppers that put everyone on their guard. People would likely stop trusting each other, and that would be disastrous for us all. That's because trust is an important ingredient for any functional society. Without it, our lives would become frustrating, tiresome, and even dangerous. Here's what a world without trust might look like…

Welcome to the Super Spooky Liars' Alternative Reality!™

Lost at an amusement park? Ask everyone you meet how to get to the front gate—can't trust only one person's opinion! Before you know it, it's closing time and you're still asking people.

There's a math test tomorrow, and even though the teacher says it covers only multiplication, you don't believe her. So you study everything you've learned all year! (Yeah. Everything.)

You're convinced you're getting less popcorn than the package says. Time to break out the scales and weigh for yourself!

Your mom doesn't trust the pharmacist to give her all the pills she bought. She counts them every time.

See? What a hassle. Double-checking everything takes way too much energy and time. It's better to keep those trust vibes strong. Not that we've ever been a completely honest bunch, though. **Check it out.** ⟶

WE'VE BEEN LYING FOR AGES...

Wow! A time machine containing a big red button with a sign that says, "Punch It"? *Of course*, you've got to take that baby for a spin. Pyramids! Knights in armor! Just don't expect to travel to an era before deception existed. People have been telling fibs—and coming up with wicked ways and treacherous tactics to catch liars—from the very beginning.

"The woolly mammoth went that way!"

Some scientists believe that lying helped our cave-people ancestor brains to grow and make us smarter! (All that extra mental hard work actually gave our brains a workout and, over time, changed us.) In other words, they believe Stone Age lying is one of the reasons we're the brainy (and deceptive) animals we are today.

Go ahead. Spit it out!

If you were accused of lying two thousand years ago in China, you might have been told to stick crushed dry rice in your mouth and chew. If you could spit it out, you were telling the truth, but if you couldn't, that meant you were afraid to be caught in a lie. Your dry mouth gave you away!

Dirty hands...and a clean conscience

To catch liars in ancient India, priests dipped a donkey's tail in black sludge and led the animal into a dark tent. One by one, suspects were sent inside to pull the "magic" tail, hoping the animal wouldn't bray—a sure sign of guilt. Emerging with dirty hands meant you had

pulled the tail (because you knew you were innocent, so why worry?). But clean hands? Anxious, you only pretended to yank. Caught in another lie—although not one you would likely be caught in again!

Which way to catch a witch?

Talk about the ultimate no-win situation. In the Middle Ages, someone accused of lying about being a witch would be loaded into a sack and thrown in a pond. If the accused liar sank and drowned, good news! She wasn't lying and was innocent. If she floated and lived, that meant only one thing: guilt (and a sentence of death). Anyone else see the flaw here?

The ultimate loophole

In the later Middle Ages in Europe, it was morally OK to lie when on trial as long as you used something called mental reservations.

What does that mean? Say you kicked a ball on Tuesday and wrecked your neighbor's cart. You could say to the judge, "I did not kick the ball," as long as you added the words "on Wednesday" in your mind. People believed that God then knew you weren't lying (because he could read your mind), and you were off the hook!

Look who's lying now

The fact that we've been interested in lying (and catching liars) since the beginning of recorded history tells us something fascinating about ourselves: Lies and deception can define us. Our lies are mirrors reflecting not only who we are as humans but what we value (hint: honesty). And although today's lies might come to us in different forms—think dishonest advertising or politicians spreading lies about their foes on TV—at their core, lies and those who tell them are the same as they've always been. And they're not going away.

DOES EVERYBODY THINK ABOUT LYING IN THE SAME WAY?

Lie. *Un mensonge.* 거짓말. Nearly every language on Earth has a word for lying. But while we all tend to agree that honesty is the best policy, the country you live in and your culture may shape some of your subtle attitudes about lies and dishonesty. So how do these differences form? Why might some cultures seem to have a relaxed attitude about lying, while others are more rigid? There's no easy answer, but here's something we do know: Our feelings about when it's OK to tell a lie can clash with our society's beliefs.

A tale of two cultures

Kids can tell us a lot about what their culture values most. That's why researchers once conducted a study with 7-, 9-, and 11-year-olds from China, Taiwan, and Canada. It went like this: The scientists read the kids a few stories. Some were about telling the truth, and others were about telling lies. Nearly all the kids knew the difference between deception and truth. Cool.

But when they were asked if it was good or bad to tell a lie, things became interesting. In one of the stories, a character did something nice for another person, but then he said he hadn't done it. He lied.

How did the kids in Canada and China react to the deception?

1. Almost all the youngest kids, no matter where they lived, said you shouldn't tell a lie no matter what.

2. The older Canadian kids generally still felt the same way: Lies are morally wrong. And anyway, why wouldn't you want the world to know you'd done a good deed?

3. Older Chinese kids tended to disagree, though. They thought it was better to lie about a good deed so that you wouldn't bring attention to it.

It's not that the Chinese kids were more dishonest than the Canadian kids. It's just that in Chinese culture, children are eventually taught in school and at home that it's important to be modest and self-effacing. It's wrong to toot your own horn. (Something North Americans have *no* problem with!) When this "modesty effect" clashes with lie-telling, Chinese kids (and grownups) may think of it not as lying but simply as doing the right thing.

I'm just trying to keep you happy, buddy

In other countries, culture also greatly impacts when people feel comfortable lying. For instance, South Koreans believe strongly in *kibun*, or saving face and keeping harmony in relationships. Making peace and getting along are so important, they might tell people what they want to hear—fib—to keep them happy.

To someone living in a Western society, where it's considered good to speak up and argue ideas, even if that means offending someone, *kibun* makes little sense. That's why things can get pretty heated when two cultures collide in, say, an international business meeting.

But now that you know how different cultures affect lies, you've got what it takes to smooth the waters with anyone you encounter, right? Bravo! Awesome! *Hyvä*!

Attitudes about lies can change

Ever heard of Anansi, the popular spider-god character from African folklore? The eight-legged arachnid is often portrayed as a trickster that uses cunning and deception. Not exactly hero material, right? But for Africans who were brought to the Caribbean as slaves, Anansi was a symbol of survival and the refusal to give up! His tricky, conniving ways helped slaves see strategies to gain the upper hand over their owners. Although most lying was considered immoral back in Africa, Anansi's lies were judged appropriate later because of the dire situation slaves were in. It was a matter of hope and survival.

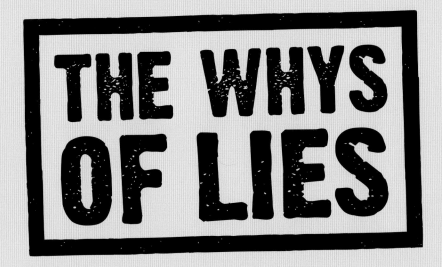

Chapter 2

THE WHYS OF LIES

TRUE STORY

"Your artwork is, well, um, er..."

Pretend you've just walked into an art gallery. Some paintings are fantastic. The others? Let's just say they're not to your taste. In fact, one of them looks like your little sister threw up all over the canvas.

But would you tell the artist who painted it how you really feel? Would you be honest or would you lie?

Me? Lie? Never!

A number of years ago, a couple of American researchers wanted to find out how many people would lie to keep from hurting a stranger's feelings. So they built themselves a very weird laboratory—a fake art gallery—and got to work.

Here's how the study went down:

Step 1. Invite people to check out your awesome new art gallery and ask them to choose two paintings they like the most and two they like the least.

Step 2. Tell them to write out exactly what they liked and didn't like about each one.

Step 3. Introduce participants to a fake "art student" (really a researcher pretending to be one) who wants to discuss the art with them.

Tell the truth? Easier said than drawn

When the fake art student said she had painted one of the favorite paintings, the participants happily explained what they liked about it. **No one lied.** Their opinions matched what they'd written down earlier. Then the student revealed she was the artist who had painted one of the disliked horrible pieces, too.

"This is the one that I did. What do you think of it?" she asked.

- Sixteen percent of people told a big, whopping lie and exclaimed they loved it!

- Only 40 percent admitted to disliking the piece.

- The rest of them tried to mislead the artist by telling subtle lies and half-truths.

People lie for many different reasons, but most lies fall into two main groups: **selfless** lies and **selfish** lies. Selfless lies, like the ones told here, protect someone's feelings. But selfish lies? We tell them to protect ourselves.

Read on and find out more.

WHY WE LIE

Reason number one: To get what we want

Ah, man! Your best friend just got a new bike, and now you're looking at your own set of wheels in a whole new light. What if you just… left your old bike at the park and told your parents it was stolen? They'd get you a new one, right? Would you really tell such a big lie? Should you? After all, you *really* want a bicycle as awesome as your friend's.

This story sheds light on the number-one **selfish** reason people lie: to get something they want. Not exactly surprising, right? But that something doesn't necessarily have to be a physical object like a bike. You might lie to get invisible things you can't touch, see, or hear.

To fit in

To feel powerful

To boost your self-esteem and feel better about yourself

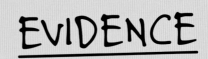
EVIDENCE

16

To buy some time

To cover up mistakes and save face

Dig deeper

Let's say that your best friend's family is wealthy and yours is not. Do you lie about what your parents do for a living? Or maybe swimming scares you. Do you tell your teacher you're feeling too sick to dive in with the rest of the class at the pool?

Hey, we've all been there. We want to show people the best version of who we are, because sometimes we're afraid no one would like the real but imperfect version. So rather than risk being teased or rejected, we lie.

"Aw, our little angel just told her first lie. We're so proud!"

Time to pass this book to your parents because this is something you'll want them to know.

Studies show us that kids begin to tell lies when they're about two or three. By four and five, they're telling whoppers, but by age seven, their biggest lying years are over. (Hopefully...)

Believe it or not, learning to lie is actually a good thing. It's related to intelligence and a sign of growing up. When you tell a lie, not only must you come up with a believable (but false) story, but your brain also has to keep track of the truth. It's what experts call a developmental milestone. Even so, smarty-pants, think twice before telling a lie.

WHY WE LIE

Reason number two: To stay safe and avoid punishment

By the time you hit kindergarten, you had probably learned four very important words:

"I didn't do it!"

Using lies to protect yourself and to avoid being punished is selfish but understandable. Who doesn't want to stay out of trouble? Isn't that a good enough reason to lie?

Extreme truth-telling

Don't tell that to people who are part of a small movement called Radical Honesty, started by American psychotherapist Dr. Brad Blanton. Followers believe people should tell the truth no matter what, even if that means getting into trouble!

But does that theory actually work in the real world? A lot of deception experts would say no. Imagine what would happen if you told your teacher you thought his tie was ugly. Or told your friend that you dislike her taste in music. In some cases, telling small, unimportant lies can actually help relationships run more smoothly and keep people from feeling hurt.

There are some upsides to radical honesty, though. You tell your secret crush how you feel and it turns out he or she feels the same way! Or you compliment your friend's beautiful flute playing and she feels more confident and happy. You feel good, too.

The bigger the risk, the bigger the lie

On a more serious note, few people would argue that lying to save a person's life is morally wrong. When put in comparison, protecting a life is more important than being branded a liar. For instance, during the Second World War, some people hid Jewish friends and neighbors and lied to German soldiers—even though that act of defiance put their families in extreme danger, too. Many would call that bravery rather than lying.

A tale of two schools

Does the threat of being punished make us more honest and less likely to lie? Canadian researchers wanted to uncover the truth, so they studied kids at two private schools in Africa.

The first school was an easygoing place. If kids did something wrong, there were consequences such as detentions, but nothing too severe. At the second school, teachers hit, yelled at, and ridiculed students for mistakes as small as forgetting school supplies. The absolute worst thing a student could do to receive this punishment? Lie.

Next, the researchers tested young students in both schools by playing the peeking game.

- Kids faced the wall while the adult pulled out a toy that made an easy-to-guess sound. (Think a crying baby doll or wailing fire truck.) Guessed right? They got a prize.

- Then the researcher brought out a silent stuffed toy cat and opened a musical birthday card. Since the card's sound had nothing to do with the toy, there was no way for students to guess the toy's identity.

- The adult left the room and told the kids not to peek. When the researcher came back, he asked them for their best guess about the toy's true identity. If kids answered "cat" but said they hadn't cheated, it was obvious they had peeked and lied about it.

So which school created the better liars? The second one. Not only did the kids lie more often, but they had learned to become excellent at it—to avoid being caught and punished!

WHY WE LIE
Reason number three: To be nice

It looks like a lie and acts like a lie, but it's told for a very different (and **selfless**) reason: to make other people feel good! That's right. Sometimes we tell a "white lie"—a small lie told to be polite or to keep from hurting someone's feelings. Luckily, studies tell us we're much more likely to tell a pack of minor or unimportant white lies than big, serious, or deceitful ones because…

There are more opportunities to tell them
We're put into many uncomfortable social situations where telling the truth would hurt someone else's feelings.

White lies are easier to keep track of
It's not like you have to come up with a complicated story. White lies are usually simple. One false statement will probably do it.

They're just not all that important
Rarely does saying, "What are you talking about? You look amazing in that lime-green suit!" come back to haunt you years later. Unless of course that friend decides to wear the hideous outfit every single day!

White lies save friendships
No one wants to be around someone who is brutally honest all the time. Ultimately, a lot of us don't always want to hear the truth. We'd rather be deceived!

Finally…

Telling small lies doesn't mess with our self-esteem

Telling tiny lies is actually a little like stealing your classmate's eraser. It doesn't seem like much of a big deal, right? It's not like you went out and robbed a bank! Only *seriously* bad people commit crimes like that, you think.

What does that have to do with small or seemingly unimportant lies? Some researchers believe humans like to feel moral even when they're not. So when they steal small items or tell little lies, it's easier to justify those actions and fool themselves into thinking they're still generally honest people. Not so easy to feel that way when stealing a car or telling big, hurtful lies, though.

But small deceptions can harm too, especially when they add up. Just imagine how you would feel if you found out your best friend not only stole your eraser, but had also been pretending to laugh at your silly jokes all year. Hurt, right?

So before telling a little lie...

...why not ask yourself if you can answer a question truthfully instead? Even small and seemingly unimportant lies can ruin a relationship over the long term. Not only might you get caught and lose trust every time you tell a lie, but you're wedging a little distance between you and the other person. There's no need to be blunt or cruel, but it's important to give people honest information when you can.

Look! My aching wing!

Even animals tell "lies" to protect other animals (and in their own animal way, be nice to them). If a predator gets too close to her nest, a killdeer bird mom will fly to another area and drag her wing on the ground, basically saying, "Hey! Over here! I'm injured and easy prey!" The predator runs after her, but she flies away. Usually, though, animals deceive to get what they want—like the devious *Photuris* firefly, which pretends to be a different species of firefly (*Photinus*) to attract a male. Once the duped firefly guy shows up, she eats him!

WHY WE LIE
Reason number four: I just can't help it!

"My dad is a billionaire with a mansion and a pool filled with molten chocolate!"

Everybody lies from time to time, but for some people, telling tall tales and fictions becomes a way of life. Even if there's no reason to make something up, they still lie anyway. But why? Researchers are still trying to sort it out. You can't just go to a doctor and find out you're a compulsive liar, because there is no official diagnosis or definition for it! People who seem to lie consistently and without reason are often medical mysteries, although they sometimes leave behind clues that give us insight into their minds. So why can't some people stop lying?

It's compulsive

Some people lie because it feels more comfortable—or even more exciting—than telling the truth. Soon, they're lying out of habit, even about any old thing, such as what they ate for breakfast (a juicy steak!) or what their weekend plans are (flying to Disneyland!).

It's pathological

The word "pathological" means you can't fully understand the consequences of your lies (say, you might hurt other people's feelings or even go to jail). You tell lies to get what you want. Period. What's more, you're great at getting people to believe you. You're often cunning, charming, and charismatic. Some pathological liars even brag that they prey on people and lie to them without feeling shame.

It's physical

If someone has a stroke or hurts his head, a blood clot can block a pathway in the brain, and suddenly that person can't tell the difference between true and false, right and wrong. He'll say anything that pops into his head, even mixing up fact and fiction in the same sentence.

It's a syndrome

Sick? Hurt? Need surgery? Too bad you're faking! Patients with Münchausen syndrome repeatedly go to the hospital and lie about phony illnesses just to get sympathy. Some sufferers are even willing to undergo risky tests and unnecessary operations. Doctors suggest it's a serious mental illness and not a cry for attention.

It's all in your head

Are seasoned liars just born that way? Back in 2005, researchers tried to answer this question by placing known liars into an MRI machine that could take super-detailed photos of their brains. They found white matter...and a lot of it, too.

Why does white matter, er, matter? Our brains are made up of two kinds of material: gray and white matter. Gray matter processes information, but white matter is like a highway that carries information—or electrical signals—to different parts of the brain. It helps us connect our thoughts and makes it easier to tell jokes, share stories...and yep, lie.

If someone has more of this brainy superhighway, does that mean she'll be a bigger liar? Not necessarily. White matter might not cause pathological or compulsive lying. It could simply mean that people who lie a lot build up more of the zippy white stuff.

Chapter 3

LIES ALL AROUND US

TRUE STORY

"Newsflash! Snakes have a ball in the ball pit!"

Maybe you've heard this story. A little kid goes to a fast-food restaurant and wants to visit the indoor play area after lunch. It has tunnels to crawl through, a swirly slide to go down, and even a ball pit to dive into.

Unfortunately, when his mom calls him out so they can go home, the boy says he's feeling sick—and there are little red marks on his skin. Eventually, he's got to be rushed to the hospital. Concerned, the mom returns to the restaurant, looks in the ball pit, and finds…a family of slithering rattlesnakes. The horror!

Don't be such a rattle-tale

Here's (very) good news: The story isn't true. It's what's called an urban legend, an untrue tale passed around from person to person and community to community. Usually the storyteller adds a few extra details or changes to make the tale seem even juicier—and more likely to be believed.

Fortunately, we know this story is an urban legend because…

Caught!

Snakes don't live in families. The moment they're born, baby snakes slip away in search of food.

Caught!

To a snake, even little kids seem terrifying, so there's no way they would want to hang out in a ball pit with them. That's the last place a momma snake would give birth to a nest of babies, too.

But the biggest hint that this story is false?

Caught!

It keeps changing! Sometimes the snakes are said to slither into ball pits at Burger King. Other times this story takes place at McDonald's. The nasty critters pop up in Texas, Louisiana, Alabama, and Arizona. They're not always rattlesnakes, either. Sometimes they are venomous copperheads, vipers, or water moccasins.

But even knowing these facts, who doesn't feel a happy little shiver of fear when being told such a story? Urban legends are popular everywhere because they're fun to tell and to hear. That they're supposed to be true and include lots of specific details, like names of real places, makes them more irresistible—and makes it harder to see them for what they really are: fiction.

So keep your eyes open. From the moment we jump out of bed in the morning until we climb back in at night, we're living with so many different sneaky lies, cheats, frauds, and deceptions, we don't even realize they're there!

Read on and see.

LIES ALL AROUND THE KITCHEN

7:00 a.m.

Good morning, sunshine! Time to grab a bite to eat before school. Before you do, though, consider the food on your plate. Are you really chomping down on what you think you are?

Maybe not. For many hundreds of years, unsavory businesspeople have tried to sell us false, unhealthy, or tainted food just to make a buck. **Food fraud**—when people lie about the food they're selling you—has a long history. Even the ancient Romans were known to sweeten wine with poisonous lead on the sly.

Got gross milk?

Let's take a slightly more recent example. Today's milk is nearly always safe to drink. It gets inspected and has been heated (pasteurized) to kill nasty bacteria. Just thank your lucky stars you weren't living through the New York swill milk scare of the 1850s, though. When the city became crowded and local pastureland grew scarce, swindlers started keeping their cows locked in dark rooms attached to breweries (places where beer is made). They advertised the drink as sweet and healthy, and said it came from pastures outside the city, even though that wasn't the case at all! The reality? They fed the city animals leftover ingredients from the brewery… then sold the "swill" (or "slop") milk that the cows produced. The nasty stuff was so watery, it couldn't even be turned into butter or cheese. It tasted a little like alcohol, too. Blegh.

It was an outrage, especially for poor families who didn't have the money to buy the healthier and more nutritious version. Many kids got sick and some even died from drinking swill milk. Eventually the liars were caught, laws were passed, and the dairies were shut down.

Nutty advertising

Since then, food producers all over the world have come under fire for selling bad food or making false claims (i.e., lying) through advertising. In one 2011 case, customers sued the company selling Nutella for promoting the nutty chocolate spread as a healthy breakfast food. The company claimed Nutella was made from healthy hazelnuts, skim milk, and "a hint of cocoa." Slather it on multigrain toast and eat with a serving of fruit, and that's one healthy breakfast. Too bad all the healthy foods mentioned in the ads weren't in Nutella. The actual main ingredients listed on the packaging? Sugar and palm oil.

The judge agreed that the company had gone out of its way to mislead people into buying and eating food that wasn't good for them. The company not only lost customers and looked bad, but it had to pay out $3 million (US).

Not so nice rice

Luckily, we're getting better at catching food fraudsters. In 2014, an English company was caught selling bags of cheap white rice mislabeled as the more expensive basmati rice. Scientists used DNA research to test it. When the fakers were caught in the act, they were charged and fined over £11,750 (approximately $18,000 US).

Eat your bugs!

Did you know that we eat a pound or two of insects each year without knowing it? (And that's even with strict regulations in place to prevent it!) But just because there's something gross on your plate, it doesn't mean you've been swindled or lied to. Remember, a liar *intends* to deceive. If restaurant owners or food manufacturers truly don't know their machines are crawling with critters, they're not being deceptive—just icky. (Hey, maybe they're even doing you a favor. Bugs are packed with protein!)

LIES ALL AROUND SCHOOL

10:30 a.m.

Dang! You forgot to study for today's spelling test. (How exactly do you spell "collywobbles" again? Oh yeah. That way.) No wonder you're feeling stressed out and even tempted to write out the words on your wrist—and cheat. Why not?

But wait!

Any time you cheat on a test or a project, you're telling a lie. By handing in that paper, you are basically proclaiming, "I worked on this project or test all by myself. These are all my ideas, and I got this mark through hard work." But that's not true.

EXHIBIT D

Cut the excuses and find reasons

It's not always easy to go cheat-free, especially if you've been cutting corners at school for a while. You might even be tempted to make **excuses**, especially if you're caught. You think, "It's a dumb class anyway" or "My teacher doesn't understand me, so why bother being honest?" Instead, figure out the **reasons** you feel you have to cheat.

Too much pressure

Does your mom get mad when you bring home a B+ on a report card? Kids who worry that they'll let their parents or teachers down feel more pressure to cheat. It's OK to tell the adults around you how you feel.

No time to study

Swimming class on Tuesday, soccer on Wednesday…It's hard to put in homework time if you're never home in the first place. Talk to your parents about decreasing your after-school load.

School is really hard

We hear you. Some subjects are challenging or maybe you're even struggling with a learning disability. You could easily be tempted to cheat just to stay caught up. Instead, ask for help from an adult who can give you the support to get back in the game.

Everybody else is doing it

It can be so frustrating to watch other kids cheat and "earn" marks that are higher than yours! According to school cheating expert Dr. Donald McCabe, 60 to 70 percent of students will cheat if they see others getting away with it. But here's something else to remember: 15 to 20 percent of students will *never* cheat.

Hey, if it worked once...

The problem with cheating is that it's like a wheel rolling down a hill. Give it a little push and it's hard to stop! Studies tell us that kids who cheat and get away with it are more likely to take the bad habit to high school, university, and the workplace. How would you feel if you found out your doctor cheated to get through medical school? Gulp.

Other evidence suggests that students who cheat and get good marks ultimately forget they're actually being dishonest. One American study showed that test cheaters were likely to deceive themselves into thinking they would ace the next test—even when they knew there was no way to cheat again!

When cheaters get an A, they feel smart and believe they're better students than they really are. In reality, they're getting further and further behind other students without knowing it. Caught in a lying loop, they're setting themselves up for a big fall when a future teacher makes cheating impossible. Suddenly it becomes obvious how little the student actually knows.

Catching the cheats

Thousands of schools and universities around the world are using computer software to make sure students aren't plagiarizing essays and papers. (Plagiarism means you are passing someone else's work off as your own—serious cheating.) In Britain alone, more than 45,000 university students were caught cheating between 2009 and 2012, partly because professors had new software to catch them.

LIES ALL AROUND WORK

2:00 p.m.

Time for Mom or Dad to take a break…a break from lying! Although most adults are honest while on the job, sometimes deception is just part of the daily routine—even if no one wants to admit it. In other cases, people tell big lies and ruin their careers.

"Here, take two and call me in the morning…"

If your doctor handed you a pill and said it would make you feel better, you'd believe her. After all, doctors take an oath to keep patients healthy. There shouldn't be any reason to lie. Except…sometimes there is. Welcome to the **placebo effect**, which is what happens when someone takes medication that he thinks will help but in reality is a big fake-out! The medication hasn't been proven to have any effect on what ails the patient.

There are different kinds of placebos. Sometimes a doctor will prescribe a sugar pill, which is exactly what it sounds like: real-looking medication made of sugar. But sometimes doctors will prescribe real medicine, even though it's not going to help a patient's particular condition. Sometimes physicians will even give "fake" shots!

Are these doctors lying? Of course they are. They're saying something that they hope will deceive the patient. In 2007, a University of Chicago study of approximately 200 doctors showed that 45 percent had prescribed a placebo at least once in their career.

Why? Placebos work about 30 percent of the time.

Sounds crazy, right? Yet loads of research shows that when some people take a pill they think will work, they feel better—because they expect to. Other studies show that placebos relax muscles and kick-start the brain's natural painkillers.

Not everyone agrees that placebos are ethical and right, and some doctors admit they're very careful not to lie outright. So rather than saying, "This is going to cure you," they will say, "This has helped some of my patients." Small change, but a big difference.

Preacher plagiarizes for profit

Some religious leaders have been caught taking other people's words, publishing them in books, and calling them their own. Some have even tried to sell the stolen sermons online! (By the way, thou shalt not do that.) It's easy to see why, though. Pastors, rabbis, priests...they need to come up with new sermons and ideas every week, and that's hard work. But because they teach honesty and truthfulness, when they plagiarize and lie about it, it seems even worse.

Bad science and lies

Science is supposed to be based on objective facts. But that doesn't keep scientists and researchers from fudging their results and lying about them. In one famous 2011 case, a Dutch professor, Dr. Diederik Stapel, revealed that dozens of his published studies were fake. He was fired from his job at the university and called "the biggest con man in academic science." (He hadn't actually discovered that eating meat makes people more selfish, for instance.)

His story made news around the world, but other scientists have also been caught fabricating and fibbing to become more famous or get better jobs. Famous stem-cell researcher Dr. Hwang Woo-Suk stunned everyone who knew him when it was revealed that almost all his research was bogus. Falsifying results seems to be on the rise, with 1 to 2 percent of scientists saying they've done it. It seems that they want what a lot of people want: to get noticed for their work.

I'M LIVING A LIE!

12:00 a.m.–11:59 p.m.

Some people's whole existence is a lie, day and night! These amazing phonies have swapped real life for a disguise to get things like money, power, or fame, or just to avoid trouble! Would you be willing to make the same trade?

Real name: Han van Meegeren
When: 1930s

Real name: Gregor MacGregor
When: 1820s

The fantastic forger

Claim to fame: This unappreciated Dutch artist decided to get revenge on art critics—by forging famous works by the iconic 17th-century painter Johannes Vermeer. They were so realistic he was able to sell six pieces for about $60 million (US). Even the Dutch government got duped at first.

Real name: Krystyna Skarbek
When: 1940s

The country crook

Claim to fame: This once-respected Scottish soldier convinced hundreds of gullible people to invest money in Poyais—his tropical paradise nation—and move there. Newspaper ads described fertile soil, warm weather, and even chunks of gold in the water. After a long journey by ship, families arrived at an empty shore and were in for a terrible shock. Poyais didn't exist! Instead, they were stranded near Belize, and many became sick and died.

The skiing spy

Claim to fame: She took on a new name, Christine Granville, and transported top-secret information back and forth between the mountains of Poland and Hungary...on skis! She even freed another spy from prison by convincing enemy soldiers she was the niece of an important military leader.

Real name: Lance Armstrong
When: 1995–2012

Real name: John C. Beale
When: 2000–2013

The hooky hoodwinker

Claim to fame: A government employee of the Environmental Protection Agency, Beale told everyone he was also a CIA agent who needed to be away from his office for months at a time. The reality? He was just playing hooky and spent his days reading, riding his bike, and doing housework...all while earning $206,000 (US) a year! After being caught, he admitted he got a "rush of excitement" from living a double life.

The bicycle betrayer

Claim to fame: The star professional cyclist wowed the world when he managed to win seven Tour de France race titles in a row. The story took a dark twist when it was discovered that he'd been taking drugs to help him ride faster. He was stripped of his titles and banned from racing for life.

All lies come to an end

Obviously, most of us who lie never let the lies get out of hand like these people did. Compulsive liars may actually get a thrill out of duping the gullible, and they can't seem to stop themselves. But those who live a lie build their fabrications like a house of cards. One wrong move...and all those cards come crashing down!

A victim of a con often:
1. is very trusting
2. loves taking risks
3. wants to feel part of a special group with secret money-making information

Chapter 4

TRUE STORY

Who Wants to Be a (Lying) Millionaire?

It was the moment everyone in the audience was waiting for. Would he answer the final question correctly? Would he win £1 million (approximately $1.5 million US)?

Major Charles Ingram was a contestant on the popular British television game show *Who Wants to Be a Millionaire?*, and in 2001 he was set to become only the third person ever to win the jackpot.

"A number one followed by one hundred zeros is known by what name?" the host asked as everyone held their breath.

Ingram looked ill. He squirmed and paused. He thought out loud and backtracked on his answers. Finally, he decided on one of four words offered—googol—despite admitting he'd never heard of the word before in his life. Talk about a leap of faith!

Or was he simply cheating?

Cough once for yes, twice for no

A week after taping the show, Ingram found out he would never be able to cash his winning check. He, his wife, and an accomplice were eventually charged with deception in court. The jury decided that an audience member, Tecwen Whittock, had coughed every time a right answer was given. It was a secret code, they concluded, and the three had hatched the plan in advance.

Other facts, however, seemed to point to their innocence. Whittock suffered from allergies and hay fever, and coughed a lot to begin with. The two men didn't seem to know each other until they had to face a judge. Although the three were eventually found guilty of cheating, detectives never did find out exactly how the Millionaire Three managed to pull off the million-dollar fraud.

Even with some evidence showing he was innocent, many people were convinced Ingram was lying.

He seemed so uncomfortable and unsure of his answers. He was restless and twitchy.

On TV, he looked like someone who was lying.

QUIZ—SPOT THE LIAR!

Think you're a pretty good judge of character, huh? Take a look at the people below. Who's lying? Who's being truthful? Can you tell just by looking at them?

Big smile

Shifty eyes

Fidgeting

DO YOUR EYES SEE LIES?

Nervous tics, shifty eyes, and shuffling feet: You might think these actions are dead giveaways that someone is being untruthful, but it turns out most of us are terrible at reading a liar's cues correctly. We tend to guess right only about 50 percent of the time, which is not much better than flipping a coin! (In other words, that questionnaire on the last page? It was a great, big trick question. Sorry...)

The wizarding world of lie detection

Some people seem to be better at lie spotting than the rest of us, but they're rare. Two American researchers, Dr. Paul Ekman and Dr. Maureen O'Sullivan, called them lie-detection "wizards." After testing 20,000 different people, they found only 50 wizards. The best of them could spot lies 80 percent of the time in three different tests.

What sets these amazing fib finders apart? They notice details most of us miss.

① **Fluttering eyelids**
When liars strongly disagree with something you just said, they might smile, but their eyelids will give them away.

② **Facial expressions**
Or they might crinkle their nose...while saying they like your new haircut.

③ **How you talk**
Liars will sometimes use more words than non-liars to say the same thing. They're also less likely to use words like "I" and "me." Instead, they place distance between themselves and the lie by using "he" or "she" and "they."

④ **Bad words**
People who swear and cuss more often tend to tell more lies, too.

⑤ **Body language**
Liars often cross their ankles, a sign of anxiety.

Being able to pick up on these cues gives wizards an edge on liars, but it's still not a perfect system.

Quick! Did you see that?

Congratulations! You just told your mom you've been nominated to take care of your school's pet ferrets over the summer. You are thrilled! What's more, your mom says she can't wait to give those feisty critters a holiday home, too. So why don't you believe her?

Maybe because you picked up on a micro-expression she didn't intend for you to see.

Researchers such as Dr. Ekman note that we give off tiny, fleeting facial expressions that we're not even aware of. How quick are they? Slice up a second into fifteen pieces, and a micro-expression uses up only one of them. Cameras can catch micro-expressions in action, but most people can't. Sometimes these expressions "leak" our true feelings about something. If you'd taken a picture of your mom's face at just the right moment, maybe this is what you would have seen.

All this may be balderdash

Just because you can see someone's expression or body language change doesn't necessarily mean they're telling you a lie. Maybe your mom is just as excited about having pets in the house as you are, but she suddenly remembered she'd left a cake in the oven and smelled it burning. Back on page 37, Major Charles Ingram's squirming may have had nothing to do with cheating the system. Perhaps he was just nervous about being on television.

Ultimately, there's no perfect system humans can use to detect lies. Maybe machines are the answer…

Or this.

Fear

Disgust

BUZZ! BEEP! YOU'RE GUILTY!

Sometimes we turn to technology to catch liars in the act. But do these truth-o-meters truly compute?

Truth-o-meter!

What: Polygraph machine

How it works: The machine measures your heart rate and blood pressure while you answer questions. Tell a lie and watch that needle jump across the paper scroll!

Fatal flaw: Polygraph machines can mistake truthful people for liars. It's possible to feel frightened or anxious, breathe fast, and have sweaty palms… even when we're innocent. (Ever feel guilty because you were worried no one would believe you?) That's one good way to trick the machine. A polygraph can detect tense feelings, but it can't necessarily detect lies.

Truth-o-meter!

What: Voice-stress analysis

How it works: Computer software looks for changes in your voice pitch (how high and low it goes) to identify if you're feeling stressed out when answering questions.

Fatal flaw: Does it work? Hard to tell. One study seemed to show that when people were told voice-stress technology was being used, they were less likely to lie.

Fake machines and real liars

Despite their poor track records, polygraph machines and other lie-detector technologies are still used on occasion. Plenty of research shows that some people will spill the beans and confess even when hooked up to a fake machine—also known as a bogus pipeline.

Truth-o-meter!

What: The P300 test

How it works: Only 300 milliseconds after a person sees a familiar image, human brain activity goes POW!!! Show a crook photos of his crime scene, and his brainwaves could give him away—no words required!

Fatal flaw: For the test to work, investigators need to find images and evidence that will trip up the bad guy. Not always easy. The person being tested must also remember many details about his crimes. These so-called guilty knowledge tests work only if the person being tested has a good memory!

Truth-o-meter!

What: Functional magnetic resonance imaging (fMRI)

How it works: Get a look directly into a liar's brain! Slide her into an fMRI machine, flip the switch, and your computer screen will show which parts of the brain "light up" when she tells a tall tale.

Fatal flaw: Not only is every brain different, but people tell all kinds of lies for all kinds of reasons. Some lies are spontaneous and told on the fly. Others are memorized and repeated over and over. Little fibs are different from mean, backstabbing lies. The brain handles all these lies in a unique way, making it impossible to come up with a straightforward method to detect lies in general.

Beat the machine!

So far, we still haven't come up with a way to catch liars, deceivers, and cheats that's 100 percent effective. In fact, new studies are being conducted to prove these new-fangled machines don't work. Something as simple as wiggling a finger or toe can sometimes defeat an fMRI machine, for example. It seems that machines, while they can pinpoint when we're feeling stressed or anxious, still have a long way to go before they can be trusted to catch us in a lie.

Truth or lie?

The polygraph's inventor is a comic book hero.

True! William Moulton Marston created Wonder Woman.

CONCLUSION

The Honest Truth about Trust

After everything you've read here about lying, cheating, forging, faking, swindling, duping, fooling, and bamboozling, who could blame you for thinking...

> "If everybody lies, why should I trust anybody?"

Here's your answer: because we're happier (and sometimes richer) if we do!

The tale of two villages

Years ago, a researcher visited two villages in Italy that were only miles apart. In terms of wealth and success, though, they could have been on opposite sides of the world. In one village, the roads were clean, houses were kept up, leaders were respected, and people were generally happy. In the second village, families struggled hard to make ends meet. There just didn't seem to be enough of anything to go around.

What was main difference between the two communities? Trust. Although some experts today think it's a controversial theory, others think there's some truth to it.

In the second, struggling village, families were very close. They trusted only the people they knew really, really well. Strangers? Forget about it. People assumed storekeepers were ripping them off, town leaders were liars, and neighbors would steal from them. In some cases, families even did bad things to other families so they could get ahead and become more successful! After a while, distrust grew. No one helped each other out or came together to make the town better, and life became harder.

GO AWAY!

Trust at home

What do Italian villages have to do with you? Well, you've probably seen what happens when trust drops in your own neighborhood. Maybe your parents recently bought a second lock for your door or put in a security system. Or maybe they worry about you walking home from school or playing outside on your own, which means you spend more time indoors.

It's harder to feel free when distrust weighs us down.

In fact, some political scientists say that communities work better when there's something called generalized trust. In other words, we trust in others, even people we don't know. Numerous studies show that when generalized trust goes up, good things happen as a whole. More people start companies and create paying jobs. Other people volunteer more and lend a helping hand to those who need it. Happiness and health even grow!

Everybody lies? Sure they do. Remember, if you believe one study, 60 percent of people can't go for more than ten minutes without lying. But you know what else? The people studied were being honest most of the time. The truth is, it's OK to be trusting. Why? Because everybody tells the truth, too.

WELCOME!

HAPPY CAFE

Index

Sources

Ariely, Dan. *The (Honest) Truth About Dishonesty: How We Lie to Everyone—Especially Ourselves*. New York: HarperCollins Publishers, 2012.

BBC News. "1957: BBC Fools the Nation." April 1, 2008. http://news.bbc.co.uk/onthisday/hi/dates/stories/april/1/newsid_2819000/2819261.stm.

BBC News. "A Brief History of Lying." January 6, 2002. http://news.bbc.co.uk/2/hi/uk_news/1740746.stm.

Bronson, Po. "Learning to Lie." *New York Magazine*. February 10, 2008.

Coughlan, Sean. "Most Parents 'Lie to Their Children.'" BBC News. January 23, 2013. http://www.bbc.com/news/education-21144827.

D'Agata, Madeleine T. "The Effect of Lying on Self-Control Depletion." Master's thesis, Queen's University. QSpace, http://hdl.handle.net/1974/8142.

DePaulo, B. M., D. A. Kashy, S. E. Kirkendol, M. M. Wyer, and J. A. Epstein. "Lying in Everyday Life." *Journal of Personality and Social Psychology*, vol. 70 (May 1996): 979–95.

Ekman, Paul. "Why People Lie." Paul Ekman Group. March 2009. http://www.paulekman.com/uncategorized/why-people-lie/.

Fallis, Don. "What Is Lying?" *Journal of Philosophy*, vol. 106 (2009): 29–56.

Greenspan, Stephen. *Annals of Gullibility: Why We Get Duped and How to Avoid It*. Westport, CT: Praegar Publishers, 2009.

Harrington, Brooke, ed. *Deception: From Ancient Empires to Internet Dating*. Stanford, CA: Stanford University Press, 2009.

Kim, M. S., K. Y. Kam, W. F. Sharkey, and T. M. Singelis. "Culture and Deception: Moral Transgression or Social Necessity?" *Communication Currents*, vol. 3 (February 2008).

Krulwich, R., and J. Abumrad. "Radio Lab: Into the Brain of a Liar." NPR: National Public Radio. March 6, 2008.

Lee, K., F. Xu, G. Fu, C. A. Cameron, and S. Chen. "Taiwan and Mainland Chinese and Canadian Children's Categorization and Evaluation of Lie- and Truth-Telling: A Modesty Effect." *British Journal of Developmental Psychology*, vol. 19 (November 2001): 525–42.

Livingstone Smith, David. *Why We Lie: The Evolutionary Roots of Deception and the Unconscious Mind*. New York: St. Martin's Press, 2004.

Pérez-Peña, Richard. "Studies Find More Students Cheating, with High Achievers No Exception." *New York Times*. September 7, 2012.

Pettit, Michael. *The Science of Deception: Psychology and Commerce in America*. Chicago: The University of Chicago Press, 2013.

University of Toronto News. "The Moral of the Story? Spare Kids Those Cautionary Tales." June 18, 2014. http://news.utoronto.ca/moral-story-spare-kids-those-cautionary-tales.

Vrij, A., L. Akehurst, L. Brown, and S. Mann. "Detecting Lies in Young Children, Adolescents and Adults." *Applied Cognitive Psychology*, vol. 20 (August 30, 2006): 1225–37.

Wilson, Andrew. "Faking It: People Who Live a Lie." *The Independent*. January 15, 2006.

Wilson, Bee. *Swindled: The Dark History of Food Fraud, from Poisoned Candy to Counterfeit Coffee*. Princeton, NJ: Princeton University Press, 2008.

Acknowledgments

To write this book, I depended on the expertise and support of so many. A big thanks goes to John Crossingham, an editor with infinite patience, a sense of fun, and the editing chops to pull a project like this together. Again. To the super-talented and charming Clayton Hanmer—a high-five. Don Fallis, professor at the University of Arizona, was willing to let me pick his brain about lying, philosophy, and ethics. This book is better for it. I'm indebted to Amy Baskin, Maxine Betteridge-Moes, Blayne Haggart, Dawn Matheson (for the writing space), Dayle Petty, and Teresa Pitman, as well as Angela Evans, Kang Lee, and Victoria Talwar for their illuminating research into lies and children. And of course, Dave, Nathan, and Nadia for everything. You're always so brilliant and helpful. That's no lie.

For Dave, who lies only to be kind. –KV

To all my friends and family who've had to sit through "stories"
of my foggy memories over the years... –CH

Text © 2016 Kira Vermond
Illustrations © 2016 Clayton Hanmer

All rights reserved. No part of this publication may be reproduced, stored in a retrieval system, or transmitted in any form or by any means, without the prior written permission of Owlkids Books Inc., or in the case of photocopying or other reprographic copying, a license from the Canadian Copyright Licensing Agency (Access Copyright). For an Access Copyright license, visit www.accesscopyright.ca or call toll-free to 1-800-893-5777.

Owlkids Books acknowledges the financial support of the Canada Council for the Arts, the Ontario Arts Council, the Government of Canada through the Canada Book Fund (CBF) and the Government of Ontario through the Ontario Media Development Corporation's Book Initiative for our publishing activities.

Published in Canada by
Owlkids Books Inc.
10 Lower Spadina Avenue
Toronto, ON M5V 2Z2

Published in the United States by
Owlkids Books Inc.
1700 Fourth Street
Berkeley, CA 94710

Library and Archives Canada Cataloguing in Publication

Vermond, Kira, author
      Half-truths and brazen lies : an honest look at lying / by Kira Vermond ; illustrated by Clayton Hanmer.

Includes bibliographical references and index.

ISBN 978-1-77147-146-6 (bound)

      1. Truthfulness and falsehood--Juvenile literature.   I. Hanmer, Clayton, 1978-, illustrator II. Title.

BJ1421.V47 2016   j177'.3   C2015-905706-X

Library of Congress Control Number: 2015948453

The artwork in this book was rendered in ink and coloured digitally.
Edited by: John Crossingham
Designed by: Alisa Baldwin

ONTARIO ARTS COUNCIL
CONSEIL DES ARTS DE L'ONTARIO
an Ontario government agency
un organisme du gouvernement de l'Ontario

Canada Council   Conseil des Arts
for the Arts   du Canada

Canadä

Manufactured in Dongguan, China, in November 2015, by Toppan Leefung Packaging & Printing (Dongguan) Co., Ltd.
Job #156333

A   B   C   D   E   F

Publisher of Chirp, chickaDEE and OWL
www.owlkidsbooks.com

Owlkids Books is a division of